ALSO BY ROSMARIE

TRANSLATIONS

The Book of Questions by Edmond Jabès
(Wesleyan University Press)

The Book of Resemblances by Edmond Jabès
(Wesleyan University Press)

The Book of Dialogue by Edmond Jabès
(Wesleyan University Press)

From the Book to the Book: an Edmond Jabès Reader
(Wesleyan University Press)

A Foreigner Carrying in the Crook of His Arm a Tiny Book
by Edmond Jabès (Wesleyan University Press)

The Book of Shares by Edmond Jabès (Chicago University Press)

The Book of Margins by Edmond Jabès (Chicago University Press)

The Little Book of Unsuspected Subversion by Edmond Jabès
(Stanford University Press)

Some Thing Black by Jacques Roubaud (Dalkey Archive)
The Plurality of World According to Lewis by Jacques Roubaud
(Dalkey Archive)

Late Additions by Emmanuel Hocquard (*Série d'Ècriture #2*)

Dawn by Joseph Guglielmi (*Série d'Ècriture #5*)

The Vienna Group: Six Major Austrian Poets
(with Harriett Watts, Station Hill)

Paul Celan: Collected Prose (Carcanet/Sheep Meadow)

With Each Clouded Peak by Friederike Mayröcker
(with Harriett Watts, Sun & Moon Press)

Heiligenanstalt by Friederike Mayröcker
(Burning Deck: *Dichten=* #1)

Mountains in Berlin: Selected Poems by Elke Erb
(Burning Deck: *Dichten=* #2)

CRITICISM

Against Language? (Mouton/Walter de Gruyter)

RELUCTANT
GRAVITIES

BY ROSMARIE WALDROP

A NEW DIRECTIONS BOOK

ACKNOWLEDGMENTS:

Parts of this book have appeared, sometimes in earlier versions,
in *Bathos Journal, Black Bread, Boxkite, Conjunctions, Colorado Review,
Diacritics, Denver Quarterly, Five Finger Review, Inscape, New American
Writing, Ohio Review, Rhizome,* and *Sulfur.*

Book design by Sylvia Frezzolini Severance, Westerly, Rhode Island
Manufactured in the United States of America
New Directions Books are printed on acid-free paper.
First published as New Directions Paperbook 889 in 1999
Published simultaneously in Canada by Penguin Books Canada Ltd.

Library of Congress Cataloging-in-Publication Data

Waldrop, Rosmarie.
  Reluctant gravities / by Rosmarie Waldrop.
    p. cm.
  ISBN 0-8112-1428-1 (alk. paper)
    1. Prose poems, American. 2. Imaginary conversations Poetry.
I. Title
PS3573.A4234R42   1999
811'.54—dc21   99-21344
                                           CIP

New Directions Books are published for James Laughlin
by New Directions Publishing Corporation,
80 Eighth Avenue, New York, NY 10011

CONTENTS

Prologue: Two Voices   1

I   Conversation 1: On the Horizontal   9
Conversation 2: On the Vertical   11
Conversation 3: On Vertigo   13
Conversation 4: On Place   15

Interlude: Song   19
Meditation on Fact   20
Song   22

II   Conversation 5: On Eden   25
Conversation 6: On Desire   27
Conversation 7: On Thirds   29
Conversation 8: On Betweens   31

Interlude: Song   35
Meditation on Certainty   36
Song   38

III   Conversation 9: On Varieties of Oblivion   41
Conversation 10: On Separation   43
Conversation 11: On Depth   45
Conversation 12: On Hieroglyphs   47

Interlude: Song 51

                     Meditation on Understanding 52

                     Song 54

IV   Conversation 13: On Ways of the Body 57

        Conversation 14: On Blindman's Buff 59

        Conversation 15: On Sharing 61

        Conversation 16: On Change 63

Interlude: Song 67

                     Meditation on the Indefinite 68

                     Song 70

V   Conversation 17: On Lift 73

        Conversation 18: On Depression 75

        Conversation 19: On Childhood 77

        Conversation 20: On Pattern 79

Interlude: Song 83

                     Meditation on Awakening 84

                     Song 86

VI   Conversation 21: On Slowing 89

        Conversation 22: On Aging 91

        Conversation 23: On Cause 93

        Conversation 24: On the Millennium 95

for Keith, always

PROLOGUE:
TWO VOICES

Two voices on a page. Or is it one? Now turning in on themselves, back into fiber and leaf, now branching into sequence, consequence, public works projects or discord. Now touching, now trapped in frames without dialog box. Both tentative, as if poring over old inscriptions, when perhaps the wall is crumbling, circuits broken, pages blown off by a fall draft.

Even if voices wrestle on the page, their impact on the air is part of their definition. In a play, for instance, the sentences would be explained by their placement on stage. We would not ask an actress what anguish her lines add up to. She would not worry what her voice touches, would let it spill over the audience, aiming beyond the folds of the curtain, at the point in the distance called the meaning of the play.

The difference of our sex, says one voice, saves us from humiliation. It makes me shiver, says the other. Your voice drops stones into feelings to sound their depth. Then warmth is truncated to war. But I'd like to fall back into simplicity as into a featherbed.

Voices, planted on the page, do not ripen or bear fruit. Here placement does not explain, but cultivates the vacancy between them. The voices pause, start over. Gap gardening which, moved inward from the right margin, suspends time. The suspension sets, is set, in type, in columns that precipitate false memories of garden, vineyard, trellis. Trembling leaf, rules of black thumb and white, invisible angle of breath and solid state.

She tries to draw a strength she dimly feels out of the weaknesses she knows, as if predicting an element in the periodic table. He wants to make a flat pebble skim across the water inside her body. He wonders if, for lack of sky, it takes on the color of skin or other cells it touches. If it rusts the bones.

The pact between page and voice is different from the compact of voice and body. The voice opens the body. Air, the cold of the air, passes through and, with a single inflection, builds large castles. The page wants proof, but bonds. The body cannot keep the voice. It spills. Foliage over the palisade.

He has put a pebble under his tongue. While her lips explode in conjectures his lisp is a new scale to practice. He wants his words to lift, against the added odds, to a truth outside him. In exchange, his father walking down the road should diminish into a symbol of age.

The page lures the voice with a promise of wood blossoming. But there is no air. No breath lives in the mouth or clouds the mirror. On stage, the body would carry the surface we call mind. Here, surface marries surface, refusing deep waters. Still, the point of encounter is here, always. Screams rise. Tears fall. Impure white, legible.

I

❋

ON THE HORIZONTAL

My mother, she says, always spread, irresistibly, across the entire room, flooding me with familiarity to breed content. I feared my spongy nature and, hoping for other forms of absorption, opened the window onto more water, eyes level with its surface. And lower, till the words "I am here" lost their point with the vanishing air. Just as it's only in use that a proposition grinds its lens.

Deciphering, he says, is not a horizontal motion. Though the way a sentence is meant can be expressed by an expansion that becomes part of it. As a smile may wide-open a door. Holding the tools in my mouth I struggle uphill, my body so perfectly suspended between my father's push and gravity's pull that no progress is made. As if consciousness had to stay embedded in carbon. Or copy. Between camp and bomb. But if you try to sound feelings with words, the stone drops into reaches beyond fathoms.

I *am* here, she says, I've learned that life consists in fitting my body to the earth's slow rotation. So that the way I lean on the parapet betrays dried blood and invisible burns. My shadow lies in the same direction as all the others, and I can't jump over it. My mother's waves ran high. She rode them down on me as on a valley, hoping to flush out the minerals. But I hid my bones under sentences expanding like the flesh in my years.

Language, he says, spells those who love it, sliding sidelong from word to whole cloth. The way fingers extend the body into adventure, print, lakes, and Deadman's-hand. Wherever the pen pushes, in the teeth of fear and malediction, even to your signature absorbing you into sign. A discomfort with the feel of home before it grows into inflamed tissue and real illness. With symptoms of grammar, punctuation, subtraction of soul. And only death to get you out.

ON THE VERTICAL

We must decipher our lives, he says, forward and back-
ward, down through cracks in the crystal to excrement,
entrails, formation of cells. And up. The way the lark at
the end of night trills vertically out of the grass —and
even that I know too vaguely, so many blades and bare-
ly sharper for the passing of blindness—up into anemic
heights, the stand-still of time. Could we call this God?
or meaning?

The suck of symbol, rather, she quotes. Or an inflection
of the voice? Let the song go on. And time. My shad-
ow locks my presence to the ground. It's real enough
and outside myself, though regularly consumed at high
noon. So maybe I should grant the shoot-out: light
may flood me too, completely. But it won't come walk-
ing in boots and spurs, or flowing robes, and take my
hand or give me the finger with the assurance of a
more rational being. And my body slopes toward yours
no matter how level the ground.

If we can't call it God, he says, it still perches on the mind, minting strangeness. How could we recognize what we've never seen? A whale in through the window, frame scattered as far as non-standard candles. The sky faints along the giant outline, thar she blows under your skin, tense, a parable right through the body that remains so painfully flesh.

So pleasurably flesh, she says, and dwells among us, flesh offered to flesh, thick as thieves, beginning to see. Even the lark's soar breaks and is content to drop back into yesterday's gravity. Which wins out over dispersion, even doubt, and our thoughts turn dense like matter. The way the sky turns deep honey at noon. The way my sensations seem to belong to a me that has always already sided with the world.

ON VERTIGO

That's why thought, he says, means fear. Sicklied o'er with the pale cast. And the feel of a woman. No boundary or edge. No foothold. Blast outspins gravity, breath to temples, gut to throat, propositions break into gasps. Then marriage. The projectile returns to the point of firing. Shaken, I try to take shelter in ratios of dots on a screen.

A narrow bed, she says. Easier to internalize combustion under a hood while rain falls in sheets, glazing a red wheelbarrow for the hell of it. I don't bait fabled beasts to rise to the surface of intonation. But I once watched a rooster mate, and he felt hard inside me, a clenched fist, an alien rock inside me, because there was no thinking to dissolve him. So to slide down, so unutterably, so indifferent.

I don't understand, he says, how manifest destiny blows
west with the grass, how the word "soul" floats through
the language the way pollen pervades tissue. Worry piv-
ots in the gut, a screeching brake, so scant the difference
between mistake and mental disturbance. Is language
our cockadoodledoo? Is thinking a search for curves?
Do I need arrowheads or dreadlocks to reach my rawest
thoughts? A keyboard at their edge?

The longer I watched, she says, the more distinctly did
I feel the snap of that shot flat inside me. So simple the
economy of nature: space appears along with matter.
So to slide down and stand there. Such self-gravity. So
narrow the gap between mistake and morning sickness.

ON PLACE

I sit in my own shadow, she says, the way my mother gave birth to it. In artificial light, blinds drawn against the darkness of power. I think of you as if you were that shadow, a natural enclosure, a world, not a slight, so I can wander through your darkness. Has our contract inverted time, made our universe contract, a cramped bed for two? And when I say your name, do I draw water, a portrait, curtain, bridge, or conclusion?

Place there is none, he quotes. Not even to hang up our archetypes. Let alone Star Spangled Banners. We go forward and backward, and there is no place. Therefore it is a name for God. My eye, steadfast on traffic lights, abolishes the larger part of the round world. I should look at my feet. Space sweeps through us, a hell of distances bathed in the feeble glow of emptiness. Outward mobility, unimpeded. Suddenly we're nobody home, without any need of inattention, imposture, or talent for deceit.

The wind whips my skin as if it were water, she says. My skin *is* water. For wind read wind, news, sky falling. Is it a mental disturbance or the higher math of love if I hear you talking under my breath and from the torn fragments assume the sun is far away and small, and a look can cause a burn? Superstition, too, is a kind of understanding, and to forego it may have consequences.

Clusters of possibilities whiz through our head, he says. Electric charges, clogged highway, screeching brakes, a house too full of guests. With grounds for disagreement and miscarriage. The light rushes in dry, screaming. But the opaque parts of the nerve oppose the noise and void the options. Then the project must be prolonged in terms of lack.

INTERLUDE

SONG

long
as in hypnosis
not easeful by half
in love

a white jug with flowers
no room
among pictures
from within

look how even of dreams
we try to make sense

MEDITATION ON FACT

"I know" is supposed to express a relation between me and a fact.

old arteries acquainted with

Where fact is taken into consciousness like your body into mine, and I'm all sponge and crevice, floating heat and sold but for the tiny point where I, instead, give birth to myself.

carrying blood
naturally

Or I stumble after, a beginning skater on thin ice. Or a hawk outlined against the sun brims my eye, the speed of steep descent its evidence.

bewitched by

This picture shows how the light falls, bright as advertising, not what stokes it at bottom. A desire comes legs apart, demanding the color red. While the hawk's plummet smears the gap visible, a scar to be deciphered as force of attraction. Or gravity.

even as far as the foot

So my relation to fact lies deep, deep below the roadbed of inquiry, below the sequence of step and foothold, vowel and consonant, diminishing with distance. Drowned under thin ice. The sun far away and small.

SONG

began gold
in the eyes
wind lifting
sheets

whispered
the classic
texts salt
in your mouth

so to slide
and slice breath

II

ON EDEN

Unreachable, she says, left of the left margin. A moment suspended. As if it didn't apply, didn't invite to bite the apple. Garden caught as in amber by an extra gravitational force. A sphere with the beauty of curved surfaces that seem flat and endless. Though it may crack. Sprung reason, hinge or nail.

Even a bold garden, he says, is already wistful. Like the bisons of the cave paintings, the phallic African gods, the frescos found in Pompeii. As if we could step into an image of what we have lost. Tight fit of pine and apple trees in turf studded with a fine fickleness of morning glories. We're not eagles soaring above, leaving every leaf as it is, but at least we don't fear flying with the sparrows. And multitudes of insects. The explicit sun, or maybe inherent wear, occults our act, and we fall back into the old tale.

Time, she says, on all sides. Without shore. We drown if we set foot in, though we're bound to. As incurably as proton and neutron are bound to the dim world of the nucleus. And once we learn to breathe in the crash of water desire rushes in, takes hold of our smallest gesture as of a sail. But at the edge of the picture we fall. And are born. In all directions.

A common nucleus, he says, but different numbers of double binds. The earth soaks up semen without drawing conclusions. A gloved finger says touch and touch me not. But who could live among ornaments wrought by abstinence? Who could be so thorough?

ON DESIRE

Don't you think it a strange coincidence, he says, that every man whose skull's been opened had a brain? And as late as 1889, Charles Brown-Sequard, a famous French physiologist, at the age of seventy-two, treated himself for waning vigor with extracts from the testicles of dogs.

What a way to bed hope, she says. With a cherished pedigree. What *I* think strange: every photo of the old house shows wide open shutters when I remember breathing gloom, the light a mere trickle from a child's pail. Of course I know which one to inhabit: memory loves hunting in the dark. The added light only exacerbates the vertigo of inner stairwells. I see you still on the first step, plucking the word "now" out of the dark thick with resistance, as if time too had forbidden chambers.

Bursts the skull, he says, the strong force coupling gluons and quarks. Flings you. And you all interval, all excess aspiring to annihilation, slip of wings, a dragonfly so transparent, so impatient to be kicked out of paradise. But the curve slackens. The crow doesn't fly as the crow flies. And it's no longer unthinkable to put on pants and trace scars on a page.

Do you think there just might be a physiological explanation? she asks. But what happens in the brain if we always relate an object to a certain difficulty? The riddle solved, the dust is supposed to settle. But if the motes keep in motion, the house under water, shadows swimming through like undeveloped photos or the inconsolable dead? A space can have this color even though light ought to be the same to all observers. The frame of memory both distinct and not distinct from looking at photographs in order to remember.

CONVERSATION 7

ON THIRDS

Opens to the touch, he says, you have to feel it, and remains as much a stranger. Fields of sesame split wide. You ride, ribcage abird, toward disappearance, toward a preorganic, duty-free state of body. As if consciousness curved into minerals, and thought, at its peak, were only a shiver.

We are afraid of each other, she says. That's why we find a makeshift mistress, a third to be excluded. Then we think we have cleared the screen, can sit crosslegged inside language and practice passion according to the Russian novel. But something, a thin fear of sundrown, remains between us, measuring the distance as if it were the essence of being close.

Like a color we don't see, but know is contained in the light? he asks. The force that couples or, if weak, revises identity and sex? Measuring distances in the mind refracts emptiness. As if we could touch the infinite when all we do is study our fingerprints on the lens. And the pain, exacerbated toward the red end of the spectrum till we're left to howl on a cosmic scale.

It matters more *how* something touches us, she says, manner more than magnitude. Even your body could bulk foreign into mine. A clinical glitch. Or the light on a clump of cottonwoods might feel like the giddier light over the Moshassuck when you know it flows miles away, or that you could take a walk inside your mind and find me there. The explanations double-lock the strangeness.

ON BETWEENS

We lie in the dunes, she says, drowned between sheets to the wind. Green capped white, the surf's disguise of beginnings, depending on the length of curve observed. If I must have a god I'll take the matter between noun and verb. The nothing that defines, shapes next-to into phrase or cleanliness. Then again, the nothing between the teeth of a comb parts nothing but the nothing between hairs. So maybe I'd rather have an old woman sprawled barefoot through fields and space foam, pushing her breasts at any weed in the world as if the only true way to see were by touch.

An intelligence that comprehends the sperm, he says. Tubes, valves transporting cells toward strange attractors, riot canals through the blood, one-way excess. Once you miss one rung of the ladder you can't stop falling. The hole takes over the argument, pigeons the sky, and the clouds, so calm a moment ago, blush and swim wild with reproduction, albeit asexual.

A space between boundary and blur, she says, a nakedness beyond male and female, edge of the sea. The tongue surrounds the mouth, so that you answer questions I failed to ask or pass sentence that has not been pronounced. The way radiation bathes the entire universe in a feeble glow and thought chases after the receding galaxies at such speed there is no question of a center and the squeeze of gravity becomes mere alibi.

But no ducts to the marrow of the mind, he says, most private part, opaque like a trauma, no fixed address. No field glasses on the firings, the real event, swerve of light. The germ of your thought swimming too deep. Endlessly in ambush, attention dissipates into longing. I listen to my thirst and know incurable's the rule.

INTERLUDE

SONG

rush of water
do not mistake
the singular
of my desire

muscle's
memory
and makeshift
mistress

incurable
the rule

MEDITATION ON CERTAINTY

The more a proposition hardens its glassy simplicity tilts all fluids away from the body, all thoughts into sudden white. A paralyzing excess of focus, and you know you'll never marry.

a third
to be excluded

Certainty so cold in the knees the words faint, amputated. The wood dries, the door starts creaking, the darkroom is opened too soon. It is the lowest point gathers. A host on the tip of the tongue equals worse than any pied piper.

here it is always
morning

The house as if you could draw your character from it, incest of immobility and sedentary adventure, breath sealed by sediment of ghosts. So inferred, daylight trickles from a high window the larger the absence of puddles on the floor.

the eye both hungry and
begins to weep

This wider lens restores confusion, fingerprints and
weeds. Relations alter. Not just the river, the bed, too,
shifts. Your mother takes a lover. Slow oscillation of lips,
as between hide and seek, magnetic and field. Speeds
red without limit through tree tops, leaves flowing
through veins.

fine hard
invisible rain

Hour of glass, pillar of salt. The words come to their
senses. It is the lowest point gathers love. Doubt, some-
times called world. It spills your heart.

SONG

we wait for rain
to fall inside
the body
like a presence of gods

so to open
so fire so silk
with fissures between
small words

in a white jug
the stem of a dream

III

ON VARIETIES OF OBLIVION

After bitter resistance the river unravels into the night, he says. Washes our daily fare of war out into a dark so deaf, so almost without dimension there is no word to dive from. Body weight displaced by dreams whose own lack promises lucidity so powerful it could shoot a long take to mindlessness. Fish smell travels the regions of sleep, westward like young men and the dawn. Then I return, too early to bring anything back, unsure of what I want, terrified I'll fail, by a hair, to seize it.

We talk because we can forget, she says. Our bodies open to the dark, and sand runs out. Oblivion takes it all with equal tenderness. As the sea does. As the past. Already it suffuses the present with more inclusive tonalities. Not orchestrating a melodic sequence, but rounding the memory of a rooster on top a hanging silence. Or injured flesh. Impersonal. Only an animal could be so.

An avatar of the holy ghost, he chuckles. Or the angel of the annunciation beating his wings against a door slammed shut. Behind it, love already plays the organ. Without the angel. He is invisible because we have rejected his message.

On the old photos, she says, I see a stranger staking out my skin. As if an apple could fall too far from the tree. Yet I call her "me," "my" years of furtively expanding flesh, with almost-certainty. It's a belief that seems exempt from doubt, as if it were the hinge on which my doubts and questions turn. Still, I may seem the same "I" to you while I've already rolled it through the next door. From left to right.

ON SEPARATION

My separation from the wetlands started even earlier, she says. In my mother's mirror, which staged dialectic on acute unease of body. There are few forest fires in the smoke, or even trains whistling, the station run down. Yet I mourn more friends than waste of trees or bald eagles lost. I carry the mirror in my occipital lobe, but cannot inhabit my womb. The silence between parts. Of speech.

A pebble in an eddy, he says, reveals the course of the current. It's in the flash of dissonance that we know, if not want, each other. A knowledge thick with green sun, parrots, snakes, charmers. Then dissolves in the rush toward the remote. I search for control, but there is only the gap to the horizon, beckoning without event.

Only out of body could we be out of time, she says. Momentarily bracket it maybe, in illness, degrees of withdrawal, flimmer above the lake. But hours reproduce. A lay in time saves the lay of the land and the garbage collects. I can't distinguish gravity from grace or other distortions of space. My now begins six billion years ago, when fish stretched their fins onto dry land, or forty, with breasts and monthly bleeding. Always already darkening, the way a sentence anticipates the period it will stiffen in.

The galaxies avoid collapsing onto each other by virtue of their recessional motion, he says. Father and son walk away from the bed in opposite directions. But sweat clings to our names steamed in the same sleep. If I withdraw to more impermeable regions, the secretions of closeness increase. As if all respiratory passages led to you. As if you were the certainty that a shadow of doubt lengthens. On my lungs.

ON DEPTH

It would take more than a pebble, she says, to plumb your undertones. Something slips away as you speak, tense with life, a startled beast in the woods. Is it a lizard, snake or bigger game? The brush closes over the trace of flight. A cloven hoof?

Isn't this a case, he says, of deep breathing pulled into spasms of interpretation the way children are pulled into the future by the gravity of their innocence? And with a speed unlimited by the young space. The joints between future and present swell and sweep apart whole galaxies. But even the most intense black still reflects a little light, and history will take care of our rage for explanation.

What if all our thinking, she says, were a search through underbrush and mud. Trying to decipher the forest without artificial light. The rustlings of language give us the illusion of a deep dimension. But our equations don't net the unknown quantity. We're only as good as our words.

Do you mean, he asks, that it's futile to ignore the bright emptiness of symbols and plunge to mine the deep? Illusory or not? The deep of focus? forest? world? the body? Where it is too dark for language to throw its shadow? Where it is not enough to know good and evil, but we must act on it, though it's beyond our strength and will destroy us?

CONVERSATION 12

ON HIEROGLYPHS

Champollion fainted, she says, once he had wrested their secret from the hieroglyphs and saw them turn transparent. The serpent no longer with power to strike, but biting its tail. I smell my salts, my packets of words, panicked. I'm no longer sure whether they shape my reality or have too little mass to interact with naked matter. Then they would pass right through the earth as I will in death.

The lightest particles gather the energy, he says, and given their density, outweigh stars. Thought follows thought, the interval calibrated on the space between your legs. Your yes fire, your no the crack of a whip. Well, more a filament breaking in a lightbulb. Eating from the Tree of Knowledge can't be undone. Only muddied, as by motivation. And the way you thrust out your belly as you walk, with almost shameless indifference, makes a void in the air, but no case for cosmic deceleration.

So even if I despair of plane surfaces, she says, writing, even talking, becomes an act of faith that my bondage to grammar and lexicon is not in vain. That these symbols in their beautiful and hallucinatory nudity blind me only to make me see. There is fire under the smoke. The sun also rises and falls.

We still read at risk, he says, but we don't need to lard the crocodile with arrows. The picture won't devour us. It is swallowed in the fluid agreements between gonads and frontal lobe at a rate relative to the dark closing in. Yet two speeds in paroxysm need not mesh. A burning heart, failing to strike while hot, may not save the burning feet.

INTERLUDE

SONG

fire tied
under your breast
all angles an apple
could fall

distances traveled
a fish to the West
the leaves blue
as the sun

it is your turn
to think

MEDITATION ON UNDERSTANDING

Even if you were to express everything that is "within you," if the flesh opened.

rain curtains
the eye

Or if it could talk, the bold insect on the page I'm reading, a moving violation pushing its smallness to the brink as exemplary economy. Pulled, as if it were one of the letters, into vain sequence by my eyes.

the surface of
a lake

Is it that I can't foresee the way your thought grows into anger? a body? How nudity is yet another garment? Blurred invasion. Can't stand in your shoes, under your wear, over your soul. Thirsty on awakening. Beside the point. The lake overflows without bringing childhood memories up into the light.

ricochets

The rings on the surface announce events already dissolving, the pebble's fluid migrations among contingent waves.

like
lovers

No deep image. A faultline through the lake. I've never dreamed of hunting though I sleep in a cave. The rain goes on falling. Rust in the bones. The riddle need not have a solution, need not be a riddle. Anyone can dream.

SONG

the king with
all his medals
rides horseback toward
the Sacred

Heart adrift
on the same wall
this is
his real life

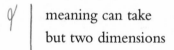 meaning can take
but two dimensions

IV

CONVERSATION 13

ON WAYS OF THE BODY

In important ways, he says, the ways of the body, speaking in one's imagination cannot be compared to crying out loud, or only like tennis with a ball and tennis without one. Yet the games are similar. This is why the idea of another world can still net a sunlit slope when the valley is already dark and we should reach for a glass of wine. Grist of images. But ordinarily I don't think of "inner events" shadowing my speech. Just as I don't worry if my sperm have long or short tails.

And what can writing not be compared to? she asks. Having a ball? A child growing from your long-tailed sperm? A boatload of foreigners climbing the Statue of Liberty, waving flags? The price of deciphering seems to be transparency. Also called fainting. The wings of the dragonfly are beautiful, but the body is not itself. I want the missing meat, bone, metabolism and ratios of heat and hunger. At the price of windows muddied with fingerprints.

Thinking runs between speech and above pigeonholes, he says, but our one sky falls on the street, leaving puddles. I worry beads between my fingers and how to revive dead letters. Or does a flower out of rubble say less for life than how meager our claims? The image is consumed in the missing detail, the gap of promise. But suddenly a word gets down on all fours and sniffs at your crotch. Or a memory screams on your cheeks while you try to hold on to the edgy afternoon.

The dog, she says. There is always a dog. But this warm flick of a tongue. Grass softer than sleep, and the dog standing over me, panting, penis flaming red from under his yellow coat and crooked as though in pain. Warm flick of tongue on my face. Wet shock. Worried boundary or bone.

ON BLINDMAN'S BUFF

Was I frightened by what I saw, she asks, or by my own eyes? Red, crooked penis. Did my hand follow its logic into blindman's buff? Did I learn to read in order to purge incomprehensible desires? A prisoner of memory regenerating in the marrow, the red power of a dog, or the stranger need of language? Missing transport by muscle or metaphor. So that I bite my lip and see beside the point.

Are you saying that greater density attracts more matter? he asks. Of fact? That abstract means distance? That our parents' act has exploded the present indicative? Nothing has ever been deciphered but turned out beasts coupling. Even books spot with secret menstrual blood and propagate their species. My hand forms letters of unambiguous design. Or are you preparing me for new ways of behavior?

Old ways, she says. Though sometimes I feel you less as an animal than huge rampant vegetation taking root inside me, covering my whole world, from top to there's no bottom, with sheer presence. And me almost bursting out of my skin, a drop of water, all surface tension. Now I spread more like a puddle, my body relaxing away from me, no matter how firmly I decline its offers of expansion.

Does it even make sense to say "then" and "now," he asks, when our world expands in every direction away from itself and the speed of light is measured to be the same regardless of how we are moving? Maybe it's the frame that strikes resemblance until the fullness of time allows all forms to dissolve? I know, aging is not an article of a woman's religion. Every night, we cover our nakedness to dry the ink. Every morning the page is as empty as the scene of a crime.

ON SHARING

Why is it, she asks, that we cannot share experience, not even under the same sheet? Rain falling or not. That my pleasure in your pleasure is unsteady like decaying atoms or continents mapped on a dream? The light of difference sharper than the warmth of next to or the same wild cucumber vine. We expected pursuit to close on happiness. But it remains pursuit, the happiness intermittent, a meteorite igniting as it passes through our air.

Any text crumbles, he says, even if we approach the tree before the leaves are falling. And the gaps don't let the light show through, let alone the color of quarks. The photographer says smile as if an unease with family likeness could be refocused as identity. In spite of superhuman efforts to keep my dead father's body from encroaching on mine, I am caught, moon in eclipse, an eager atom weighing toward form out of sheer need for anxiety.

Intermittent, she says, as if a space of time, too, could not be occupied by two bodies. Even bodies of experience and memory. As if we had no history, only a past purloined by nothing to show for it. The way I feel robbed in the morning, dreams bleached by the rush of too bright light. A film gone white, with only stray bits of raw dark. The body inhabits those as consciousness inhabits forgetting. And the gap between pain and knowing recloses the way matter comes to in the light.

Our love moved with the slowness of an object, he says. Blueshifted as sitting for a portrait where you can't grudge time. It awakened fingers at the tip of our words, chambers in the heart. Then suddenly everything too close, a splinter under the skin. The model has gotten a cramp, the cat eaten her young. Vertigo of reflections, the smooth surface lost in eddies and currents.

ON CHANGE

A splinter lodged in the brain, he says, this effort to trap fluctuations in wavelength or feeling. To see not only both duck and rabbit in the puzzle, but to freeze the moment of flip. Or a moment of aging. Is it too subtle, like grass growing, like the size of a proton? Or is our inability more categorical, the way a shadow cannot catch the light, or the eye see its blind spot? Do I love your face because it is yours or because of the way it differs from circle, parabola, ellipse?

Perhaps we need change to see what's there, she says. And ambiguity, to be aware of seeing. Seven types of apples. But focus on the curvature of the lens, and night gains all color, torpor all deeds, even their reflections in the river. Pores stop their doors. The grass is blunt with mass, the sky not infinite, just soot.

echo of "Seven Types of Ambiguity"? intentional?

So we should not watch each single breath, he asks, but simply take in the world and hold it in our body? With the roots laboring in the ground? with poplars standing straight and stiff in the acid rain? And breath by breath set it down again and not worry how *is* connects with *the case?* Like an acrobat? An acrobat.

There are things, she says, we cannot say. But to keep them down in the body doesn't save us. Even if use equals meaning, nakedness may not rise to the occasion of high noon. Legend says time began when an eagle pierced the sun and was consumed in fire. Moment of transfiguration, sublime and pitiful. The mind suffering sunstroke, overcome by its own light just when it thinks it is defeating the darkness.

INTERLUDE

SONG

we practice
the body
with moldy bread
with holes in the cheese

so to decipher
or feel
the thinning
under the skin

is there still time to act
on impulse

MEDITATION ON THE INDEFINITE

If a pattern of life is the ground for using a word the way tree bark beds columns of ink, then the word must contain some penumbra, some pulp, some that is never born.

the shape of smoke

Life is, after all, collusion of thick and fast, spacetime foam and Berenice's hair, curving suddens, sand, surds, masses of matter. Nonplussed. No exact exchange. Swords.

muscles endeavor
to shorten

Sharper concepts would not pack lunch. Sharper eyes not see farther than irregularities of wave and too wet. Not their own blind spots. Born as an afterthought I doubt propositions without body heat or shadow.

vague terms

We can predict high-pitched storms, but not the wind's local practice. Opposing thumb and upright imposture. What people will and. Distress blowing cold, inches of slow disguise.

replaced by waves

Polymorph appearances and singular gods. Five is a hand, ten a whole perversion. Pretending to recognize the relatives as if to make amends. For refusing progeny. If our universe.

sets us
guessing a proper
game

SONG

in this country
the orphans
are tall
and pollen is carried by wind

if a girl stands
a baby
hooked to her hip
what takes the place of

little enough
counts the change

V

❈

ON LIFT

I used to think, if I were light enough my conjectures would take wing, he says. But it's for the birds, the emptiness in the bone, the compulsion to keep moving: air affords no perch, gravity not neutralized by neighboring particles. And the light stays just beyond the upper left corner, not weighed down into substance by a lead pencil or the ridiculous mouse I expect to give birth to mountains.

"The act of writing weakens the eyes, bends the back, breaks the ribs, cramps the belly. It's a pox on the whole body," said a cranky copyist in the eleventh century, she says. We already carry too much equipment on our back to carry a tune up the mountain, what with thin air. And the weight makes us sluggish to move, even to open our shutters. So there are many things we do not see. And what if we saw the enormous woman collapsed on the sidewalk? We can't leave her lying there. But she is much too heavy to lift.

Odd, he says, how the road to our neighbor tends to run parallel, past her, out into emptiness. I'd like a space where we would *have* to intersect. Or else be hyperbolically myself, alone and too tall. As a book may be a book only if, once the voice has abandoned it along with daylight, it is still worth its candle. I lost my father by following him at a mathematically precise interval. Given how young the universe, you could deliver a child and never recover it.

From birth, she says, we breathe against the mark. Half the girls want to be boys; half the boys, birds. Bright tail feathers over soft lift of flesh. An extra ledge for song, a soar of pleasure to invent the world. Fewer sing every spring. Meanwhile my body expands horizontally, stretching the distance between my breasts to incomprehension.

CONVERSATION 18

ON DEPRESSION

What if sense disintegrates even though you're stroking my breasts? she asks. If I can't put my arms around you, the gesture hollow like a bad actor's? If words abandon me? If I find emptiness where you find yourself, and it's neither sheltering nor sky? If my eye no longer holds things in the way of a lover, flesh offered to flesh, or even a task? If it shirks and shrinks back into its orb of blind bone, opens and closes only to let empty light travel through?

The steady breeze levels the ridges in the sand, he says. Though it leaves specks of mica. Instead of a handful of world we find too many material structures, even if biodegradable, with flavors strange and charmed. Quarks and leptons proliferate, clouds of gas, polluted light, and dogs fight over the shadow of a bone. Not to mention trademarks and other corporate black magic. Yet the eye's not a black hole, no matter what its color. Uncluttered by things, it sees inward, into the heart. Which of course may also be empty.

Are you telling me there's no hope? she asks, that I'm dark matter that doesn't emit or reflect radiation? Or to clear out the gossip of perception, so even minimal attention can span a paradigm? The way a change of light, or love, can reveal a face? Or erase it? The way the leaden stupor of extreme fatigue can sometimes weigh toward a lucidity so keen it cuts?

Shrinking cores and exploding peripheries, he says. Supernovae, new Crab Nebulae. A stricken star, but, ah, a lovely light, rose window, chandelier. Perhaps light is only the consciousness of the dark? Like the quick, brilliant flash when the sleep cable snaps and leaves us bereft, stripped of we don't even know what, when we would at least hold the promised hand.

ON CHILDHOOD

I've had no childhood, he says. Small body, yes, small arms, small mouth, small eyes. Small noise of stomach, lips. Small talk. But how greedily my mother loved more iridescent feathers. Tossed into thin air I madly flapped my shimmering identities to nerve fear into buoyancy. But my flutter did not sustain flight. Her rocking did. An interruption, and I fell.

No flight simulation in my childhood, she says. A muted, almost prenatal state with folded membranes, webbed in waiting. A fierce desire, though, to scale the mountains, bald as they were, the craggy blocks of shale and slate, harsh, brittle, all downward pull, crumbling the time I was blind to. They held up a deep space of promise that widened the eye toward horizons of a different color, toward a crucial indifference out of all bounds.

In the first grade I wore a black apron, he says, on which my chalky fingers left their alphabet, so many hieroglyphs that would not be deciphered. It seemed to pull me toward being a girl. When I lifted it over my head, between me and the sun, I became an apprentice blackboard, a smooth slate on which words and things played their shellgame.

A girl's space, she says, and I might add, a scientist's, would be more like foam, or sponge, a structure of wormholes and maybe bridges. Not this excess of black and white, of words in profile, with birds' heads pointing the direction to read them. Toward the death of a childhood you remember but can no longer decipher. Only a written language can die, all others disappear without a trace.

ON PATTERN

I wouldn't want to accuse you of imperfection, she says. Your way of looking at things seems to dress patterns, master ceremonies. You walk as through a formal garden, an inner music cadencing your steps, and all paths intersect. Whereas I shlepp on swollen feet, arms scratched by perhaps imagined brambles, through a wilderness where roads disappear, where even riverbeds wander. And the point vanishes.

The point of music is constant vanishing, he says, and don't mistake pattern for paradise. My world seems a random scatter of snapshots pretending innocence rather than an epiphany of face. We want to believe a focus on light clarifies, if at the price of harshness. But a century of looking through the ultimate keyhole has leached the revelation from under covers and drawn blinds. Now all we've got is a bald mountain.

Or, she says, standing here at the foot of the stairs as if they were an exit, maybe *I'm* what's vanishing, to the point of a figment in someone else's story, feverish. Then my arrogant first person singular would limp in a dichotomy of virtual and existence. All I think, so many commas and periods, dry air, an Arabia Deserta of the mind. With a whiff of smoke reserved for the gods. A pain so flawless you stop breathing. Tacit turns, not on the scale of the voice.

When you speak of pain, he says, it remains hidden under the rush of phonemes, less singular than their sequence and seal. But at least the words, showy as flowers flaunting their sexual parts, save us from the eye's illusion of immediate knowledge where, once the lesions examined, the window is undressed and nobody home. In the aftermath, I cannot enter. I carry photos of my absent loves but don't set a place for them at the table.

INTERLUDE

SONG

small body small
talk
so adult
a sadness

the song of less birds
maps the land
a ghost of surface
resting on oil rigs

sleep is a stranger's glove
and the cold comes through

MEDITATION ON AWAKENING

The air vibrates with occult alphabets and the sun's rays
bend over a book, but the world is dark. Then one day
I open my seeing eye, and there is a dog.

morning admits
no impediment

I'm not sure what's to be done with this picture. Or the
dog.

a mirror
complicates

Clearly, we must explore. How the eye blinks a ladder
out of oblivion and a step beyond, to see the imaginary
depth of the mirror invade the body. Where it folds
into letter size.

no soft to the touch
without detour

Exquisitely specific antibodies sidetracked by desire. The light turns to matter, the metaphor gray. The body, jubilant to meet its double, bites into the apple.

upper limit speed

The Book open in the middle of the kitchen will protect the house from lightning. The dog will burn.

though to consciousness
nothing
can happen

The pictures seem to save us work, check the sentence through to the period. But will it wait into the small hours? For words to fall into my mouth, fresh snow on snow already fallen?

SONG

What is the
key of loss?
A face
erased?

absence
so porous
only a woman
can inhabit

sun far away and small
the water in the jug evaporated

VI

ON SLOWING

Even if our life seems scattered, a text always going astray, it builds on constants, she says. Like a piece of music. The mind should be able to embrace it in its full extravagance and touch the architecture of cause even as it forms. More so with the years, with resources of slowness. You must sit in a blue shift to sort seed from going to.

Not sit, he says. Arrows toward new setting out even as the day sets. It's in walking, albeit more slowly, that I find where I need to go, just as following the seduction of one basic rule can unknot the dimensions of a whole system. When I try to pace my breath's hovering potential with the wind, particles form into perspective and ride out into the large. I charter a ship, then try to understand what I had in mind.

You launch exotic birds, she says, and some adapt to the Rhode Island winter. I stick with domestic varieties, crows in my face, a rooster on the brain, maybe a Rhode Island Red. Such simple desire blasting the bones electric, so matter of fact, to perch on crags and cliffs. But highs are only one element of the climate. The shadow of a cloud, and my breasts droop, faintly mournful. The sun drops. The surface of the leaves turns blue.

Cells rusts, he says, not hunger. It seems yesterday that, gasping with shock, I plunged into the January river for the unreachable that is promised—though only as long as we have no history. Now the train's speed is hostage to the next station, becalmed legs and thinning hair. Could it be that loss completes possession? Becomes, like the "with" in "without," a second acquisition, deeper, wholly internal, more intense for its pain?

ON AGING

Take the hordes of children, she says. So to take off on the crest of light, so to dash toward the horizon through bushes and kneehigh grass, undeterred by stop signs, fences or decapitated statues. As if waking were as liquid and hospitable as sleep. As if games didn't close into fistfights. As if innocence were forever, though time might age, and whole seasons forget to be born.

Even children, he says, toss their pebbles across the river to throw off some undefined unease that weighs on them. As does the indifference the stones drop into. But for a moment their call and echo from bank to bank barely touch the water, skip as on light, as into regions of enhanced density, ever increasing in power.

So was it war or games or clockwork that sped our
growing up? she asks. Or simply the way particles
behave in a field of force? One day the girl disappears
into a different point of reality, a woman with sagging
breasts. And still my sense of self remains woolly as in
sleep, as if the years had only heaped on more blankets.
I always want to hear the sirens, albeit tied to the mast,
but I fear becoming the sailor with ears plugged, just
plugging away at the oar.

Penelope isn't part of your scenario? he asks. No
needlework to undo the fire feeding on our cells? Your
woolly self still makes me get under the blankets. But I
too want to get down, through the roar and twang, to
the deep horizon note I know is there though I can't
hear it: my own frequency, my way of being in the
world. Is this another image that holds me captive? So
deep in the grain I have no way to reach it? And if I
could? I once saw a dog stray into the subway and hit
the live rail.

CONVERSATION 23

ON CAUSE

I step into my mother's room, she says, and though a woman's body is a calendar of births and injunctions to death, time disappears. Only dead enough to bury could prove sound to silence or the anxiety I know by heart and lung. In my mother's room. The tie between us anticipates any move to sever it. Terror and lack of perspective. The river runs clear without imparting its clarity, whether we step into it or not.

Deep in the bones, he says. If a butterfly fluttering its wings in China can cause a storm in Rhode Island, how much more the residues of radiation, family resemblance and past rituals. The stove glows red. Thin apple trees line the road. You think you are taking a clean sheet of paper, and it's already covered with signs, illegible, as by a child's hand.

The heart has its rhythm of exchange, she says, without surplus or deficit. Mine murmurs your name while conjugating precise explosions with valves onto the infinite. I take it down with me, in the body, to develop in a darkroom of my own. The way the current elongates our reflection in the river and seems to carry it off.

A death without corruption is the promise of photography, he says. Focus and light meter translating a cut of flesh into a tense past laughing its red off. But the film's too clear. Even if smudged with fingerprints. Even if the light falls into the arms of love.

ON THE MILLENNIUM

There are many invisible borders, she says. Some erect and inexorable like death or when a lover recedes into friend. But how we fuss as we approach the millennium, after having dozed in its secular sense so long. As if civilization were drawing its lazy length up into a moment of moments, where Human-Nature-Can/Cannot-Be-Changed would slide down opposite slopes of time. The horizon is a function of eye-level. Are we not nose to the ground, overestimating things Christian?

A frame supports what would, on its own, collapse, he says. When I say "book" you don't think clay tablets, silk scrolls, or palm leaves strung together. And deep focus can make the ground turn figure the way light is the coming-to of the dark. In retrospect. Like a German sentence that comes clear only once you reach the verb at its end. By a strong effort of will. Time divides us into dust, but also binds our bodies forward. Though the exhaustion will not be squared.

The moon is constant, she says, my bleeding, a calendar. The instant we apprehend an end we desperately predict new wagon trains to head West, as if adding zeros could create bluer skies and more self-evident truths. As if the universe could big-bang again. And again. When even the most moderate increase in gravity would, instead, make it disappear. Too many dots per inch. Machinery whirring while the credit's gone.

Writing pulls East, he says, like the ground under our feet. For all our love of speed we cling to the slower proofs measured in mutations, milky ways, and ever the wind blows. Poof. The spectacle inside the eye projects its large rhythm onto a trust in daybreak. Which we make ours. Because as long as we follow we lag behind, and the centuries pass intestate.

New Directions Paperbooks—A Partial Listing

Walter Abish, *How German Is It.* NDP508.
Ahmed Ali, *Twilight in Delhi.* NDP782.
John Allman, *Scenarios for a Mixed Landscape.*
  NDP619.
Alfred Andersch, *Efraim's Book.* NDP779.
Sherwood Anderson, *Poor White.* NDP763.
Wayne Andrews, *The Surrealist Parade.* NDP689.
David Antin, *Tuning.* NDP570.
G. Apollinaire, *Selected Writings.*† NDP310.
Jimmy S. Baca, *Martin & Meditations.* NDP648.
Balzac, *Colonel Chabert.* NDP848.
Djuna Barnes, *Nightwood.* NDP98.
J. Barzun, *An Essay on French Verse.* NDP708.
H. E. Bates, *A Month by the Lake.* NDP669.
  A Party for the Girls. NDP653.
Charles Baudelaire, *Flowers of Evil.* †NDP684.
  Paris Spleen. NDP294.
Bei Dao, *Old Snow.* NDP727.
Gottfried Benn, *Primal Vision.* NDP322.
Adolfo Bioy Casares, *A Russian Doll.* NDP745.
Carmel Bird, *The Bluebird Café.* NDP707.
Johannes Bobrowski, *Shadow Lands.* NDP788.
Wolfgang Borchert, *The Man Outside.* NDP319.
Jorge Luis Borges, *Labyrinths.* NDP186.
  Seven Nights. NDP576.
Kay Boyle, *The Crazy Hunter.* NDP770.
  Fifty Stories. NDP741.
Kamau Brathwaite, *MiddlePassages.* NDP776.
  Black + Blues. NDP815.
William Bronk, *Selected Poems.* NDP816.
M. Bulgakov, *Flight & Bliss.* NDP593.
  The Life of M. de Moliere. NDP601.
Frederick Busch, *Absent Friends.* NDP721.
Veza Canetti, *Yellow Street.* NDP709.
Anne Carson, *Glass, Irony & God.* NDP808.
Joyce Cary, *Mister Johnson.* NDP631.
Hayden Carruth, *Tell Me Again. . . .* NDP677.
Camilo José Cela, *Mazurka for Two Dead Men.*
  NDP789.
Louis-Ferdinand Céline,
  Death on the Installment Plan. NDP330.
  Journey to the End of the Night. NDP542.
René Char, *Selected Poems.* †NDP734.
Jean Cocteau, *The Holy Terrors.* NDP212.
M. Collis, *She Was a Queen.* NDP716.
Gregory Corso, *Long Live Man.* NDP127.
  Herald of the Autochthonic Spirit. NDP522.
Robert Creeley, *Windows.* NDP687.
Guy Davenport, *7 Greeks.* NDP799.
Margaret Dawe, *Nissequott.* NDP775.
Osamu Dazai, *The Setting Sun.* NDP258.
  No Longer Human. NDP357.
Mme. de Lafayette, *The Princess of Cleves.*
  NDP660.
Debra DiBlasi, *Drought.* NDP836.
Robert Duncan, *Selected Poems.* NDP754.
Wm. Empson, *7 Types of Ambiguity.* NDP204.
S. Endo, *Deep River.* NDP820.
  The Samurai. NDP839.
Caradoc Evans, *Nothing to Pay.* NDP800.
Wm. Everson, *The Residual Years.* NDP263.
Lawrence Ferlinghetti, *A Coney Island of the Mind.*
  NDP74.
  These Are My Rivers. NDP786.
Ronald Firbank, *Five Novels.* NDP581.
F. Scott Fitzgerald, *The Crack-up.* NDP757.
Gustave Flaubert, *A Simple Heart.* NDP819.
J. Gahagan, *Did Gustav Mahler Ski?* NDP711.
Forrest Gander, *Science & Steepleflower:* NDP861.
Gandhi, *Gandi on Non-Violence.* NDP197.
Gary, Romain, *Promise at Dawn.* NDP635.
W. Gerhardie, *Futility.* NDP722.
Goethe, *Faust,* Part I. NDP70.
Allen Grossman, *Philosopher's Window.* NDP807.
Martin Grzimek, *Shadowlife.* NDP705.
Guigonnat, Henri, *Daemon in Lithuania.* NDP592.
Lars Gustafsson, *The Death of a Beekeeper.* NDP523.
  A Tiler's Afternoon. NDP761.
Knut Hamsun, *Dreamers.* NDP821.

John Hawkes, *The Beetle Leg.* NDP239.
  Second Skin. NDP146.
H. D. *Collected Poems.* NDP611.
  Helen in Egypt. NDP380.
  Selected Poems. NDP658.
  Tribute to Freud. NDP572.
  Trilogy. NDP866.
Herman Hesse, *Siddhartha.* NDP65.
Susan Howe, *The Nonconformist's Memorial.*
  NDP755.
Vicente Huidobro, *Selected Poetry.* NDP520.
C. Isherwood, *All the Conspirators.* NDP480.
  The Berlin Stories. NDP134.
Lêdo Ivo, *Snake's Nest.* NDP521.
Fleur Jaeggy, *Last Vanities.* NDP856.
Henry James, *The Sacred Fount.* NDP790.
Gustav Janouch, *Conversations with Kafka.* NDP313.
Alfred Jarry, *Ubu Roi.* NDP105.
Robinson Jeffers, *Cawdor and Medea.* NDP293.
B. S. Johnson, *Christie Malry's. . .* NDP600.
G. Josipovici, *In a Hotel Garden.* NDP801.
James Joyce, *Stephen Hero.* NDP133.
Franz Kafka, *Amerika.* NDP117.
Mary Karr, *The Devil's Tour.* NDP768.
Bob Kaufman, *The Ancient Rain.* NDP514.
John Keene, *Annotations.* NDP809.
H. von Kleist, *Prince Friedrich.* NDP462.
Dezsö Kosztolányi, *Anna Edes.* NDP772.
Rüdiger Kremer, *The Color of Snow.* NDP743.
M. Krleža, *On the Edge of Reason.* NDP810.
Jules Laforgue, *Moral Tales.* NDP594.
P. Lal, *Great Sanskrit Plays.* NDP142.
Tommaso Landolfi, *Gogol's Wife.* NDP155.
D. Larsen, *Stitching Porcelain.* NDP710.
James Laughlin, *The Secret Room.* NDP837.
Lautréamont, *Maldoror.* NDP207.
D. H. Lawrence, *Quetzalcoatl.* NDP864.
Siegfried Lenz, *The German Lesson.* NDP618.
Denise Levertov, *Breathing the Water.* NDP640.
  Collected Earlier Poems 1940–60. NDP475.
  The Life Around Us. NDP843.
  Poems 1960–1967. NDP549.
  Poems 1968–1972. NDP629.
  Sands of the Well. NDP849.
  The Stream and the Sapphire. NDP844.
Harry Levin, *James Joyce.* NDP87.
Li Ch'ing-chao, *Complete Poems.* NDP492.
Li Po, *Selected Poems.* NDP823.
C. Lispector, *Soulstorm.* NDP671.
  The Hour of the Star. NDP733.
  Selected Crónicas. NDP834.
Garciá Lorca, *Five Plays.* NDP232.
  Selected Poems. †NDP114.
  Three Tragedies. NDP52.
Michael McClure, *Simple Eyes.* NDP780.
Carson McCullers, *The Member of the Wedding.* (Playscript)
  NDP153.
X. de Maistre, *Voyage Around My Room.* NDP791.
Stéphane Mallarme,† *Selected Poetry and Prose.*
  NDP529.
Bernadette Mayer, *A Bernadette Mayer Reader.* NDP739.
Thomas Merton, *Asian Journal.* NDP394.
  New Seeds of Contemplation. NDP337.
  Selected Poems. NDP85.
  Thoughts on the East. NDP802.
  The Way of Chuang Tzu. NDP276.
  Zen and the Birds of Appetite. NDP261.
Henri Michaux, *A Barbarian in Asia.* NDP622.
  Selected Writings. NDP264.
Henry Miller, *The Air-Conditioned Nightmare.* NDP302.
  Aller Retour New York. NDP753.
  Big Sur & The Oranges. NDP161.
  The Colossus of Maroussi. NDP75.
  A Devil in Paradise. NDP765.
  Into the Heart of Life. NDP728.
  The Smile at the Foot of the Ladder. NDP386.
Y. Mishima, *Confessions of a Mask.* NDP253.
  Death in Midsummer. NDP215.
Frédéric Mistral, *The Memoirs.* NDP632.

For a complete listing request free catalog from
New Directions, 80 Eighth Avenue, New York 10011   †Bilingual

Eugenio Montale, *It Depends.*† NDP507.
   Selected Poems.† NDP193.
Paul Morand, *Fancy Goods/Open All Night.* NDP567.
Vladimir Nabokov, *Nikolai Gogol.* NDP78.
   Laughter in the Dark. NDP729.
   The Real Life of Sebastian Knight. NDP432.
P. Neruda, *The Captain's Verses.*† NDP345.
   Residence on Earth.† NDP340.
   Fully Empowered. NDP792.
New Directions in Prose & Poetry (Anthology).
   Available from #17 forward to #55.
Robert Nichols, *Arrival.* NDP437.
J. F. Nims, *The Six-Cornered Snowflake.* NDP700.
Charles Olson, *Selected Writings.* NDP231.
Toby Olson, *The Life of Jesus.* NDP417.
George Oppen, *Collected Poems.* NDP418.
István Örkeny, *The Flower Show/*
   The Toth Family. NDP536.
Wilfred Owen, *Collected Poems.* NDP210.
José Emilio Pacheco, *Battles in the Desert.* NDP637.
   Selected Poems.† NDP638.
Michael Palmer, *At Passages.* NDP803.
Nicanor Parra, *Antipoems: New & Selected.* NDP603.
Boris Pasternak, *Safe Conduct.* NDP77.
Kenneth Patchen, *Because It Is.* NDP83.
   Collected Poems. NDP284.
   Selected Poems. NDP160.
Ota Pavel, *How I Came to Know Fish.* NDP713.
Octavio Paz, *Collected Poems.* NDP719.
   A Draft of Shadows.† NDP489.
   Selected Poems. NDP574.
   Sunstone.† NDP735.
   A Tale of Two Gardens. NDP841.
   A Tree Within.† NDP661.
Victor Pelevin, *The Yellow Arrow;* NDP845.
   Omon Ra. NDP851.
Ezra Pound, *ABC of Reading.* NDP89.
   The Cantos. NDP824.
   Confucius. NDP285.
   Confucius to Cummings. (Anth.) NDP126.
   Diptych Rome-London. NDP783.
   Guide to Kulchur. NDP257.
   Literary Essays. NDP250.
   Personae. NDP697.
   Selected Cantos. NDP304.
   Selected Poems. NDP66.
Caradog Prichard, *One Moonlit Night.* NDP835.
Eça de Queirós, *Ilustrious House of Ramires.* NDP785.
Raymond Queneau, *The Blue Flowers.* NDP595.
   Exercises in Style. NDP513.
Mary de Rachewiltz, *Ezra Pound.* NDP405.
Raja Rao, *Kanthapura.* NDP224.
Herbert Read, *The Green Child.* NDP208.
P. Reverdy, *Selected Poems.*† NDP346.
Kenneth Rexroth, *An Autobiographical Novel.* NDP725.
   Classics Revisited. NDP621.
   More Classics Revisited. NDP668.
   Flower Wreath Hill. NDP724.
   100 Poems from the Chinese. NDP192.
   100 Poems from the Japanese.† NDP147.
   Selected Poems. NDP581.
   Women Poets of China. NDP528.
   Women Poets of Japan. NDP527.
Rainer Maria Rilke, *Poems from The Book of Hours.*
   NDP408.
   Possibility of Being. (Poems). NDP436.
   Where Silence Reigns. (Prose). NDP464.
Arthur Rimbaud, *Illuminations.*† NDP56.
   Season in Hell & Drunken Boat.† NDP97.
Jerome Rothenberg, *Khurbn.* NDP679.
   Seedings & Other Poems. NDP828.
Nayantara Sahgal, *Rich Like Us.* NDP665.
Ihara Saikaku, *The Life of an Amorous Woman.*
   NDP270.

St. John of the Cross, *Poems.*† NDP341.
W. Saroyan, *Fresno Stories.* NDP793.
Jean-Paul Sartre, *Nausea.* NDP82.
   The Wall (*Intimacy*). NDP272.
P. D. Scott, *Crossing Borders.* NDP796.
   Listening to the Candle. NDP747.
Delmore Schwartz, *Selected Poems.* NDP241.
   In Dreams Begin Responsibilities. NDP454.
W. G. Sebald, *The Emigrants.* NDP853.
Hasan Shah, *The Dancing Girl.* NDP777.
C. H. Sisson, *Selected Poems.* NDP826.
Stevie Smith, *Collected Poems.* NDP562.
   Novel on Yellow Paper. NDP778.
   A Very Pleasant Evening. NDP804.
Gary Snyder, *The Back Country.* NDP249.
   Turtle Island. NDP381.
Gustaf Sobin, *Breaths' Burials.* NDP781.
Muriel Spark, *The Comforters.* NDP796.
   The Driver's Seat. NDP786.
   The Public Image. NDP767.
Enid Starkie, *Rimbaud.* NDP254.
Stendhal, *Three Italian Chronicles.* NDP704.
Antonio Tabucchi, *Pereira Declares.* NDP848.
Nathaniel Tarn, *Lyrics . . . Bride of God.* NDP391.
Dylan Thomas, *Adventures In Skin Trade.* NDP183.
   A Child's Christmas in Wales. NDP812.
   Collected Poems 1934–1952. NDP316.
   Collected Stories. NDP626.
   Portrait of the Artist as a Young Dog. NDP51.
   Quite Early One Morning. NDP90.
   Under Milk Wood. NDP73.
Tian Wen: *A Chinese Book of Origins.* NDP624.
Uwe Timm, *Invention of Curried Sausage.*
   NDP854.
Charles Tomlinson, *Selected Poems.* NDP855.
Lionel Trilling, *E. M. Forster.* NDP189.
Tu Fu, *Selected Poems.* NDP675.
N. Tucci, *The Rain Came Last.* NDP688.
Paul Valéry, *Selected Writings.*† NDP184.
Elio Vittorini, *A Vittorini Omnibus.* NDP366.
Rosmarie Waldrop, *A Key into the Language of America.*
   NDP798.
Robert Penn Warren, *At Heaven's Gate.* NDP588.
Eliot Weinberger, *Outside Stories.* NDP751.
Nathanael West, *Miss Lonelyhearts & Day of the Locust.*
   NDP125.
J. Wheelwright, *Collected Poems.* NDP544.
Tennessee Williams, *Baby Doll.* NDP714.
   Cat on a Hot Tin Roof. NDP398.
   Collected Stories. NDP784.
   The Glass Menagerie. NDP218.
   Hard Candy. NDP225.
   A Lovely Sunday for Creve Coeur. NDP497.
   The Roman Spring of Mrs. Stone. NDP770.
   Something Cloudy, Something Clear. NDP829.
   A Streetcar Named Desire. NDP501.
   Sweet Bird of Youth. NDP409.
   Twenty-Seven Wagons Full of Cotton. NDP217.
   Vieux Carre. NDP482.
William Carlos Williams. *Asphodel.* NDP794.
   The Autobiography. NDP223.
   Collected Poems: Vol. I. NDP730.
   Collected Poems: Vol. II. NDP731.
   The Collected Stories. NDP817.
   The Doctor Stories. NDP585.
   Imaginations. NDP329.
   In The American Grain. NDP53.
   Paterson. Complete. NDP806.
   Pictures from Brueghel. NDP118.
   Selected Poems (new ed.). NDP602.
Wisdom Books:
   St. Francis. NDP477; *Taoists.* NDP509;
   Wisdom of the Desert. NDP295.
Yūko Tsushima, *The Shooting Gallery.* NDP486.

For a complete listing request free catalog from
New Directions, 80 Eighth Avenue, New York 10011

†Bilingual